AMERICAN TRAVELER

PENNSYLVANIA

SMITHMARK

This edition first published in 1992 by SMITHMARK
Publishers Inc., 112 Madison Avenue,
New York, New York 10016

ISBN 0-8317-0501-9

Printed and bound in Spain

Writer: Bob Brooke
Designer: Ann-Louise Lipman
Design Concept: Lesley Ehlers
Editor: Sara Colacurto
Production: Valerie Zars
Photo Researcher: Edward Douglas
Assistant Photo Researcher: Robert V. Hale
Editorial Assistant: Carol Raguso

Title page: A lone cannon stands in mute
testimony to the thousands of Civil War
soldiers, both Union and Confederate,
who died on the battlefield of Gettysburg.
Opposite: The Benjamin Franklin Bridge,
named for Philadelphia's favorite son,
soars high above Penn's Landing, the city's
revived waterfront promenade.

They came in droves—Swedes, Welsh, Germans, English, and French—bringing with them their own unique belief in God. Together they forged a new life and eventually a state that has become a microcosm of America.

Since the days of its founding by William Penn, Pennsylvania has been a mecca for nonconformists and social experimenters. The keystone of the 13 original colonies, hence its nickname "The Keystone State," it typifies the America that was a magnet for so many immigrants. From 1643, when Swedish colonists first came to Tinicum Island in the Delaware River, Pennsylvania has always attracted those in search of a better life.

Pennsylvania, as a formal colony, was not organized until 1682. To collect a large claim he had against the English crown, William Penn, a Quaker, asked Charles II for a grant of land in the New World where Quakers and other nonconformists could live with freedom of religion. Penn set up his colony near what is now Chester. The land was purchased from the Native Americans with such fairness that all lived in peace and harmony until 1755, the start of the French and Indian War. Penn chose Philadelphia, meaning "City of Brotherly Love" and the same name as that of an early Christian city in Asia Minor, for the name of his new city.

Generally, the early settlers chose names for their towns that reminded them of their homelands or took the names Native Americans had already given them—Punxutawney, Hollsople, Wilmerding, Hop Bottom, and

Preceding page: It once was an unwritten law that no Philadelphia building should rise higher than the hat brim on the statue of William Penn that adorns City Hall; now several sleek highrises soar beyond that height, transforming Philadelphia into a modern city. *This page, top:* Philadelphia's new skyline rises high above the statue of a Gettysburg soldier also standing in front of City Hall. *Right:* One Liberty Place has become a symbol of the "new" Philadelphia, setting the tone for what the city could ultimately become.

Claes Oldenburg's steel sculpture *Clothespin* is one of Philadelphia's most familiar landmarks. *Below:* One of the many squares in Penn's "Greene Countrie Towne," Rittenhouse Square is the site of numerous cultural events, including the city's largest outdoor art show, and continues to be the center of high society in Philadelphia. *Opposite:* The contrast between old and new Philadelphia can be seen in the old Reading Terminal Building, now being converted into the city's new convention center, and the striking ARA Building, which stand side by side.

Wapwallopenwaht, for example. Few other states can boast post offices in places with such intriguing names as Shicksshinny or Loyalsock, Normalville or Neshaming. Puzzletown, Applevold, and Forty Fort are all part of the 15,000 towns and villages crammed into the state's 45,000 square miles.

The first to settle in Penn's colony were English Quakers. They were followed by a large number of Welsh, who are credited with naming Radnor, Gwynedd, and Bryn Athyn, among other towns, and with whom the established Swedish colony later merged. Next came the Germans, who settled in Germantown, north of Philadelphia, and established the first manufacturing center in the New World.

The Pennsylvania Dutch—from the description of themselves as *deutsch*—were soon followed by the Scotch-Irish, the descendants of Scots who had settled in Northern Ireland. Strengthened by Penn's ideas and the laws he devised to make them a reality, Pennsylvania quickly became a formidable commercial center, using the ports on the Ohio River, Lake Erie, and the Delaware River to trade with Europe and the other colonies.

Pennsylvania has always been a state of firsts. Pennsylvanians established institutions that would become an integral part of America's cultural life: the first lending library, first zoo, first university, first newspaper, and first savings bank. The first fire-fighting company, the Union started operating in 1736 and the Pennsylvania Hospital opened in 1751. In 1846, the first commercial

Top: One of the five original squares in the city, Logan Circle displays an ornate Alexander Sterling Calder fountain decorated with allegorical representations of Philadelphia's three rivers. *Left:* A reproduction of Auguste Rodin's *The Thinker* stands outside the newly renovated Rodin Museum, which contains the largest collection of the artist's sculpture and drawings outside France.

Another favorite sculptural Philadelphia landmark is Robert Indiana's *Love* along John F. Kennedy Boulevard. The steel sculpture, with its distinctive crooked "O," has been appropriately declared the greatest acquisition of the City of Brotherly Love. *Below:* The Franklin Institute Science Museum is a hands-on museum where visitors can pilot a jet plane, ride a 350-ton steam locomotive, walk through a giant human heart, or explore the future through the science and technology of the twenty-first century.

This contemporary sculpture stands at the entrance to the Philadelphia Museum of Art, the third-largest museum in the country featuring more than 500 thousand priceless paintings, drawings, and prints. *Below, left:* A giant marble statue of Benjamin Franklin at the Franklin Institute is a constant reminder of the dreams of discovery and invention he brought to Philadelphia. *Right:* A bronze statue of Justice John Marshall stands in front of the neoclassic portico of the Philadelphia Museum of Art.

...legraph was used between Philadelphia and Lancaster. The first commercial broadcasting station in the world, KDKA in Pittsburgh, went on the air in 1920.

Pennsylvania was also an early transportation hub. The state hitched its wagon to the railroads long after the Conestoga wagons (which also began here) ceased to ply the first turnpike, between Philadelphia and Lancaster. The first railroad in America was a wooden-railed affair at a quarry not far from Philadelphia. The Pennsylvania Railroad was chartered in 1852, and soon thereafter the Lehigh Valley, Reading, Erie, and Cumberland railroads provided fast service for people and freight into every state bordering Pennsylvania. By the turn of the century, 60 major railroads moved across the state.

The first Pennsylvanians found every conceivable kind of terrain in this temperate region. Half of Pennsylvania is covered in forests, of both hardwoods and conifers. The state's great range of plant life includes species that normally grow in other regions. It also has a diversity of wildlife, although some of the larger animals, such as moose and elk, disappeared in the days when logging and hunting were unregulated. Today, Pennsylvania undertakes extensive reforestation programs and has reintroduced vanished species to the wilds.

Pennsylvania's earliest residents were farmers. The overlays of limestone soil in some parts of the state made farming an extremely worthwhile enterprise. Lancaster County, in the Pennsylvania Dutch country, has outproduced any other area of equal size since its residents began farming it centuries ago.

Top: Philadelphia is a city full of statues, and none is more majestic than that of George Washington on the circle in front of the Philadelphia Museum of Art. *Right:* The museum features one of the largest collections of period rooms in the country; its American wing offers exhibits of silver, furniture, costumes, and paintings from colonial times to the present.

The Philadelphia Museum of Art rises above the restored Fairmount Waterworks; both are part of Fairmount Park, the largest landscaped city park in the world. *Below:* One of Philadelphia's most endearing landmarks is Boat House Row along the Schuylkill River; these turn-of-the-century boat houses are home to rowing teams from the city's numerous colleges and universities.

Of the more than 200 buildings constructed for the Centennial Exposition of 1876 held in Fairmount Park, Memorial Hall is the only major edifice still intact. Erected as an art gallery and intended to be permanent, the massive granite building was considered in its day to be the height of artistic elegance. *Below:* The large impressive columns at the entrance to Memorial Hall are not in any way related to the Centennial Exposition, but were constructed in 1890 to honor the city's Civil War heroes. *Overleaf:* South Philadelphia is the site of the sports complex where the city's four professional teams have established a national reputation for the city.

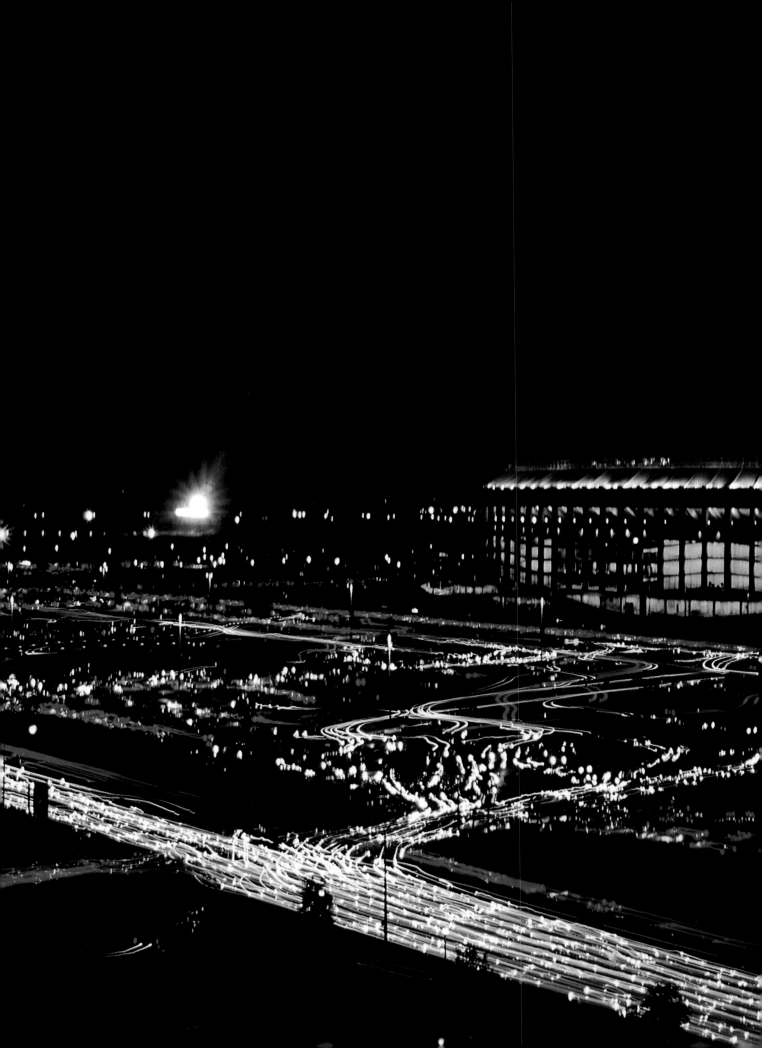

The Delaware Valley, with Philadelphia as its hub, drew the highest concentration of immigra? to Pennsylvania. Spread over the southeast corner of the state like spokes of a wheel and taking in fo? counties—Bucks, Chester, Delawa? and Montgomery—it was a mercant? and agricultural center for decade? Though its communities are losin? their pastoral character to shoppi? malls and tract housing, they are retaining their charm in their old churches, meetinghouses, fieldsto? mills and mansions, and public buildings.

These communities have not only preserved historic buildings but open spaces as well. The rollin? landscape of Valley Forge Nationa? Park has been frozen in time and appears much as it was during the heroic winter encampment of Washington's patriot army in 1777? The historic campground, howeve? is now being pressed by the bulgi? limits of Philadelphia. Around its northern perimeter flows the wide? fast-moving Schuylkill (pronounce? Skook'l) River, which is paralleled by the four-lane, faster-moving Schuylkill Expressway.

Other reminders of the Revolution also crowd this corner of Pennsylvania. Brandywine Battlefield Park, 30 miles southw? of Philadelphia, is where the Batt? of Brandywine took place on September 11, 1777. In that battl? Washington and his outnumbered army tried unsuccessfully to preve? the British from taking Philadelph? This is also the home of the Brand? wine school of artists, where Howa? Pyle, Newell Convers Wyeth, and Andrew Wyeth painstakingly recorded life in the countryside around them.

Top: The location of the First Bank of the United States from 1791 to 1811, this building now houses the offices of Independence National Historical Park ? well as changing exhibits. *Left:* Carpent? Hall was the meeting place of the First Continental Congress in 1774; it is now? historical museum with exhibits of early? tools and artifacts, including the Winds? chairs used by the Continental Congress?

The portrait gallery of Independence National Historical Park is housed in the Second Bank of the United States in Old Philadelphia. *Below, left:* Often called "the most historic square mile in America," Independence National Historical Park is filled with prominent sites and tributes to the founding of our nation. *Right:* Some of the city's finest buildings were at one time devoted to government and religion, and they are, for the most part, the ones that still dominate Old Philadelphia.

The countryside north of Philadelphia is a patchwork of mellow vistas. Bucks County, lying along the Delaware River, is filled with natural charm overlaid with a lot of history. People have gone to Bucks County to escape the bustle of Philadelphia and New York for years. Writers and artists were drawn to wooded New Hope in the early twentieth century, and by the 1930's, when the railroads replaced the Delaware Canal, had established a thriving colony. Stagecoach stops, inns, and taverns provided lodging for travelers in early times; today, the towns that sprang up around them are following in the tradition by offering accommodations in restored inns and charming bed and breakfasts.

Above New Hope is a photogenic world of wooded hillsides that drop steeply to dark and cool valley floors where clear streams chatter briskly or softly murmur on their way to the Delaware River. Farther inland, the Bucks countryside is dotted with villages where stone houses and whitewashed barns sit by rushing creeks in settings that evoke the spirit of days gone by.

Even the heart of Philadelphia has its open space. The oldest and largest city park in America, Fairmount Park, an 8,000-acre reserve where William Penn's idea for a "greene countrie towne" seems to have been fulfilled, stretches for several miles over the hills along both sides of the Schuylkill River and the Wissahickon Creek.

Top to bottom: The Governor's Council Chamber, on the second floor of Independence Hall, is where the early governors of the 13 colonies met. The Supreme Court Room is where the Provincial, later the Pennsylvania, Supreme Court met until the middle of the nineteenth century. The Committee of Assembly Room is where the Declaration of Independence was signed; the quills are silent, but the aura of history has not faded. *Opposite:* Originally constructed between 1732 and 1756, Independence Hall was the site where the Second Continental Congress declared independence from England; where the Articles of Confederation were drafted; and, later, where the U.S. Constitution was penned.

The park was the site of the Philadelphia Centennial Exposition in 1876. When the fair closed, a whole truckload of artifacts, in 42 freight cars, was shipped to Washington for display in the Smithsonian. Plants and shrubs were moved to nearby Longwood Gardens. The sculpture of an arm holding a torch, called the "Statue of Independence," was moved to Madison Square Park in New York to wait for the rest of the figure to which it would be attached; the completed figure was then placed in the harbor there and renamed the Statue of Liberty.

Most Americans know Philadelphia's "old city" as the birthplace of the nation. Here, Independence National Historical Park, the most historic square mile in America, provides a well-groomed setting for some of the country's most famous old buildings, including Independence Hall. Although skyscrapers now pierce the skies above William Penn's statue on City Hall, Philadelphia is a handsome and revitalized core where open space is abundant and the mellow look of former times has returned. Only one street remains, however, that truly retains the cramped scale of the 1700's: Elfreth's Alley, just off Independence Park near the river, is a six-foot-wide cobblestone lane that looks like the setting for a Dickens novel, its tiny houses huddled against each other as if for support.

West of Philadelphia, near Lancaster, is the stronghold of the world-famous Pennsylvania Dutch. German in origin, they are descendants of religious refugees from the

Preceding page: The Liberty Bell, our country's most hallowed symbol of freedom and liberty, stands in its own glass-enclosed building. *This page, top:* Patriots, loyalists, heroes, and traitors have all worshipped at Christ Church, the congregation of which was organized in 1695. *Right:* Located directly across from Independence Hall is one of Old Philadelphia's most prominent landmarks, the Bourse; once a thriving nineteenth-century business exchange, it is now a retail and office center.

Elfreth's Alley is the oldest residential street in the United States, with homes dating from between 1725 and 1835. *Below, left:* This restored eighteenth-century home and upholstery shop is furnished with many of Betsy Ross's personal possessions and displays that depict her life as a flagmaker, upholsterer, and patriot. *Right:* The museum at 126 Elfreth's Alley is filled with period furnishings and changing exhibits.

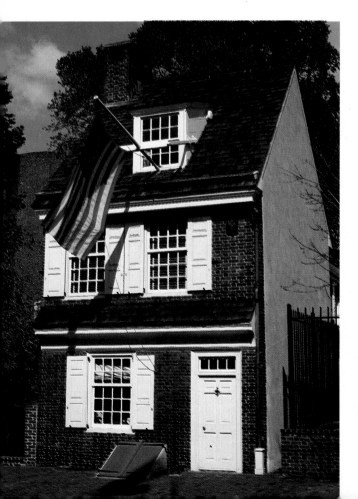

The Great Plaza at Penn's Landing hosts a myriad of concerts and festivals that celebrate the ethnic heritage of Philadelphia. *Below:* What is believed to be the site of the original house occupied by William Penn in the early days of Philadelphia is now a peaceful neighborhood park. *Following page:* The maritime history of the nation and of the Philadelphia area is represented by historic ships permanently anchored at Penn's Landing; each is a floating museum.

Preceding page: The Philadelphia Exchange, architect William Strickland's 1834 Greek Revival masterpiece, served for 50 years as the site where merchants gathered to barter and sell their wares. *This page:* The cobblestoned streets of Society Hill reflect the historic nature of the area. *Below, left:* The Dickens Inn is a familiar landmark on Head House Square, one of Old Philadelphia's earliest market squares. *Right:* Society Hill's Sephardic synagogue of the Congregation Mikveh Israel, dating from 1740, housed Philadelphia's first Jewish congregation; nearby is its burial ground, where such notables as Rebecca Gratz, who was given enduring life as the heroine of Sir Walter Scott's *Ivanhoe,* are buried. *Opposite:* Head House Square is lined with brick row houses that now serve as restaurants and shops.

hineland who came to Penn's
beral land in the early eighteenth
ntury to practice their beliefs in
ace. The Pennsylvania Dutch have
stablished themselves as the world's
est farmers in some of the world's
est farming country. The Germanic
fluence is strongest in the small
wns of Hamburg, Kutztown, and
mmaus, and in the bigger ones of
llentown, Reading, and Lebanon,
ome of a sausagelike food known
s "Lebanon bologna."

In Pennsylvania Dutch country,
e religious sect observing the
rictest practices is the Amish. The
ty of Lancaster has some farmer's
arkets where the Amish come to
ll their produce, the women wearing
eir distinctive bonnets, the men
ith their beards and broad-brimmed
ats. The merchants and their
roduce arrive by horse and buggy,
r the Amish disdain the technology
the twentieth century.

As far back as 1815,
ennsylvanians have retreated
the Pocono Mountains in the
ortheast part of the state to enjoy
e scenery and to hike and ride the
arrow mountain trails. Lower in
titude than some of the more
emote ridges in the state, and a lot
mer, the Poconos are filled with
kes, adding a fresh, cool ingredient
the pine-scented air even on the
ottest days. More recently, the
ildlife of the Poconos has had to
are its environment with ski
thusiasts, who flock to the slopes
ke geese during the winter.

Early fur trappers were the first
discover the Susquehanna Valley
central Pennsylvania. This is an
z-like landscape of mountainous

receding page: The Old Original
ookbinder's, one of the nation's most
opular seafood restaurants, serves up live
aine lobsters, Columbia River salmon,
mbo soft-shell crabs, and fresh bouillabaise
nd chowders a short distance from the
elaware River. *This page, top:* The cast-
on facades of buildings in the Old City
ection of Philadelphia are being restored
nd painted with bright colors. *Right:*
ouses along Eighth Street reflect the
olonial style of architecture found
roughout the Society Hill section.

ridges, rolling plateaus, quicksilve
streams, and the grand river that
rolls through its heart like an arte
that keeps things in good working
order. The Susquehanna River is
indeed the lifeblood of the rugged
interior. Navigable only by shallow
draft vessels, it is nevertheless a br
water-carrier, being a mile wide in
its lower reaches around Harrisbur
Its beautiful Native American nan
means "muddy river."

Harrisburg, on the east bank
of the Susquehanna at the edge of
mountain country, was originally
used by trappers as a ferry stop an
trading post. The town itself was
officially established in 1785 by th
son of the original founder of the
post, after whom it was named
Harris' Ferry. Its strategic position
brought it into contention for the
new nation's capital, but Washingt•
was chosen instead. It became the
Pennsylvania state capital in 1812

Harrisburg's crowning touch
is its ornate Italian Renaissance
capitol building, its dome rising
majestically from the high perspec
tive of hills behind the river. The
city's quiet good looks remain toda
a combination of natural gifts and
careful planning. Its broad river
drive lined with big old trees and
magnificent homes gives it a regal
dignity.

Milton Hershey's ancestors
emigrated to central Pennsylvania
in 1717 from Switzerland. They
belonged to the Swiss Brethren, wl
later became known as Mennonite:

Top: Pennsylvania's State Capitol in
Harrisburg, a massive 651-room granite
Italian Renaissance palace, was designed
by Joseph M. Huston; the 272-foot-high
dome was inspired by St. Peter's in Rome.
Left: The interior of the Capitol is laden
with late-Victorian works of art and floor
tiles designed and manufactured at
Henry Mercer's Moravian Tile Works
in Doylestown.

The town of Hershey is dedicated to chocolate, as seen in the Hershey Kiss street lamps lining Chocolate and Cocoa avenues. *Below:* The Hershey Museum of American Life, founded by Milton Hershey, is dedicated to American history and folk art and features first-rate collections of Pennsylvania–German folk art and Native American artifacts.

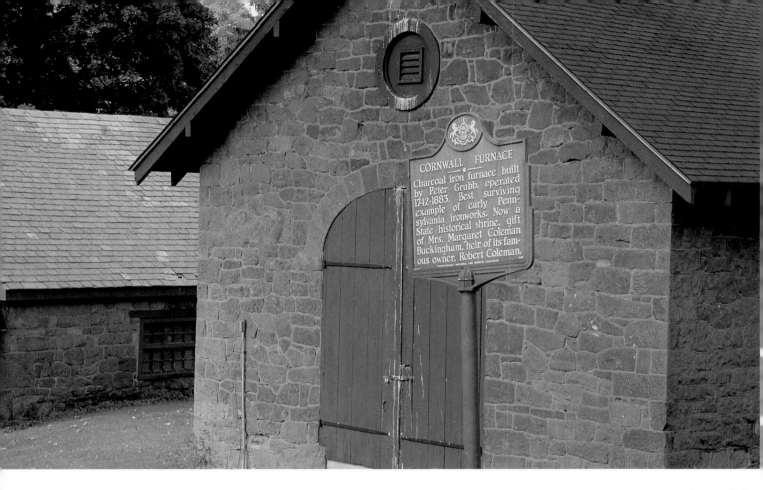

The Cornwall Iron Furnace is a well-preserved sandstone foundry and stone furnace where pig iron was made between 1742 and 1883. *Below, left:* The large stone furnace at Cornwall was unusual for its size and was used to make iron for cannon during the Revolutionary War. *Right:* The ironmaking process, using charcoal as fuel, is explained in exhibits throughout the complex. *Opposite:* The village of Intercourse, in the heart of Pennsylvania Dutch country, is ablaze with bright orange pumpkins at Halloween.

Intercourse, along with Bird-in-Hand and Paradise,
are well-known Amish villages just east of Lancaster.
Right: Neat Amish farms dot the countryside near
Intercourse.

The Strasburg Railroad is the oldest short-haul railroad in the country and now travels back and forth between East Strasburg and Paradise, a 9-mile, 45-minute round trip. *Below:* The engines used on the Strasburg Railroad are steam, of course, and both these and the coaches date from the late 1800's.

Hershey got the idea for making his famous chocolate candy using real milk at the Columbian Exposition of 1893. The town he built around his highly automated factory was named after him.

Civil War devotees stand in awe when they visit the battlefield at Gettysburg, where the climactic battle of the Civil War was fought on July 2, 3, and 4, 1863, and where Lincoln gave his stirring address. In that battle, the North and South were locked in mortal combat and for 50,000 men, Gettysburg was the last battle. Some 2,300 monuments grace the 16,000 rolling acres here, many of which have been beautifully restored to their original appearance.

Some 80 years earlier, during the Revolutionary War, the first members of the Continental Congress sought refuge from the British in nearby York, founded in 1741. The ridges of the Tuscarora and Blue mountains stretch for miles like giant waves following one upon the other. In long views across the blue-green valleys, the land merges with a hazy purple horizon.

Central Pennsylvania is little-known territory punctuated by wilderness. Larger towns such as Williamsport, a former lumber center, Sunbury, State College, and Lewistown are absorbed into their river or mountain settings with no noticeable loss to the lush charms of the natural background.

In this mountainous region farming is still an active occupation. The towns are minor interruptions in the midst of rolling fields of corn and wheat. Along the highway, their clapboard, brick, and stone houses

Top to bottom: The impressive brick Romanesque Revival Central Market in Lancaster is the fourth building on the site since 1742 and is still in use as a market. The 1874 Soldiers and Sailors Monument in downtown Lancaster was originally intended to commemorate Civil War dead; it now also honors those who died in other military conflicts. Wheatland, the home of President James Buchanan, a native of Lancaster and America's only bachelor president, is a Federal-style brick mansion purchased by Buchanan in 1848; he lived there until his death in 1868.

The symmetry of Pennsylvania Dutch barns is outlined against the sky near Lancaster; hex signs, painted on the barns, were at one time believed to ward off evil spirits. *Below:* Amish haystacks, like huge jelly rolls, line the fields at harvest time near Paradise.

uggle close to the street, wide
orches running along their fronts
nd sometimes around the sides.
ellow-looking red brick churches
nd unobtrusive shops are found in
wn centers. The sidewalks are
arrow and the main streets curve
nd dip to follow the rolling land-
ape. These are friendly places
here everyone says hello.

State College, also known as
niversity Park, is home to the
ittany Lions of Penn State
niversity, nationally famous
otball heroes. Nearby, Bellefonte,
hose town name means "beautiful
untain" in French, is nestled
gainst Bald Eagle Mountain.
upposedly the French statesman
allyrand named it while on a visit
ere during his exile from France
1794. The town's Big Spring still
urs forth 11 million gallons of
re, cold mountain water daily.

One of the state's most remark-
le natural formations, the "Grand
anyon of Pennsylvania," winds
rough 300 thousand acres of
restland near Wellsboro. Fifty
iles long, it drops 1,000 feet as it
ts through Pine Creek Gorge. On
isp fall days, the steep forested
alls of the chasm are resplendent
gold and scarlet. The red-tailed
awk is king here, its echoing cry
ingling with the splash of the
shing creek. The area's autumn
lors are in part a legacy of the
ew Englanders who settled in
orth-central Pennsylvania in the
te eighteenth century, determined
annex the region to Connecticut.

p to bottom: Wheat sheafs line the
ables at Ephrata Cloister, formerly a
erman pietistic community of sisters
nd brethren. Founded by German pietist
ystic Conrad Beissel in 1732, Ephrata
as patterned after medieval religious
mmunities in the Rhineland; demonstra-
ons of old crafts such as candlemaking
e held periodically in this once totally
lf-sufficient community. The Pennsyl-
nia Farm Museum of Landis Valley,
aturing 22 exhibit areas interpreting
ral farm life before the turn of the
ntury, is one of the most impressive
useum–village complexes in the country.

They planted their elms and sugar maples in the countryside and raised houses in the New England style, with Greek Revival columned porticos.

Beyond the Allegheny Mountains lies western Pennsylvania, America's first bitterly contested frontier region. Here the French and Indian War was fought over Fort Dusquesne, later renamed Fort Pitt by the British, which still later became the city of Pittsburgh. The state's second-largest city after Philadelphia, Pittsburgh is one of America's major ports. In fact, more tonnage passes through Pittsburgh per year than travels through the Panama Canal, giving way to huge fortunes.

The western side of Pennsylvania has, like the east, played a crucial role in the state's development. Geographically, historically, and economically it has long been a keystone area of the Keystone State. The business prominence that came about in the nineteenth century was due to the mineral and fossil-fuel wealth of the region.

In the 1840's, immense deposits of bituminous coal were discovered west of the Alleghenies. Mined from enormous veins, the coal fed industry's energy appetite until 1859, when Pennsylvania-grade oil, a high-quality lubricating oil of unsurpassed excellence, was discovered by Edwin Drake at Titusville. By the turn of the century, Pennsylvania's wells produced 60 percent of the nation's oil.

Preceding page: An Amish family walks along a country road outside Lancaster. *This page, top to bottom:* A bronze statue of Conrad Weiser in Homestead commemorates his role in keeping the peace between the Iroquois and white settlers between 1737 and 1750. The Daniel Boone Homestead, outside Birdsboro, represents what the home of the Boone family may have looked like in the mid-1700's; the original cabin was dismantled, a few portions of which were incorporated into the present fieldstone house. The Hopewell Village National Historic Site near Elverson is probably the best example of an ironmaking community in the country; most of the restored and reconstructed stone and frame buildings have the appearance they assumed in the 1820–40 period.

The Lehigh Parkway in Allentown is part of one of the most extensive city park systems in the country. *Below:* A mountain stream tumbles through Ricketts Glen State Park west of Scranton, in the heart of the Pocono Mountains of northeast Pennsylvania.

Longwood Gardens, located 30 miles southwest of Philadelphia in the Brandywine River Valley, was formerly the country estate of Pierre S. du Pont; the conservatory is the scene of numerous musical events throughout the year. *Below:* Longwood's 350 acres of indoor and outdoor gardens and woodlands display 14,000 different kinds of plants, including numerous seasonal flowers; from mid-June through August, Longwood heralds its annual Festival of Fountains, when hundreds of jets shoot cascades of water as high as 130 feet into the air.

Chadds Ford is best known as the home of the
Wyeth family of painters, but it was also the site of
the Battle of Brandywine in 1777. *Right:* Although
threatened by suburbanization, the countryside of
the Brandywine Valley has retained its bucolic charm.

Pittsburgh, many say, is the beginning and end of all that happens in western Pennsylvania. The city at the confluence of the Three Rivers—the Allegheny, the Monongahela, and the Ohio—is the centerpiece of the region. Its vitality as a city has come from great waves of ethnic groups—Germans, Lithuanians, Serbs, Hungarians, English, Scots, Irish, and Italians—that have come together to create a city of great drive and enormous confidence in its abilities. The Golden Triangle, symbol of Pittsburgh's industrial and financial might, rises sharply etched in the newly scrubbed air on the point of land formed by the converging Allegheny and Monongahela rivers. As twilight falls on the city, the curtain rises on a cultural extravaganza of symphonies, ballets, and theater.

Pittsburgh's strategic position astride two rivers and at the head of a third, and its equally strategic position as a gateway to the interior of the country, started it off with a flourish on its career as a center of industry. The competition of the railroad giants—the Pennsylvania and the Baltimore & Ohio—and the activities of such business giants as Andrew Carnegie, Andrew Mellon, and George Westinghouse helped to establish Pittsburgh as a powerful center of commerce.

The iron ores of the region, now much depleted, made Pittsburgh the "steel city" in the last century. Most of the steel mills, however, have long since closed, giving way to high-tech industries, and the oil fields have yielded supremacy to the giants of the Southwest.

Preceding page: Valley Forge National Historical Park was the site of George Washington's 1777–78 winter encampment and not a battlefield, as is often believed; the National Memorial Arch, commemorating the soldiers who braved that harsh winter, was erected in 1917. *This page, top:* Other memorials in Valley Forge National Historical Park include the impressive bronze equestrian figure of General Anthony Wayne, placed on the site from where he commanded his Pennsylvania troops. *Right:* National Park Service rangers dressed in the uniforms of Revolutionary War soldiers stand in front of one of the restored log soldiers' huts.

Preceding page: A bronze statue of George Washington stands watch over the fields of Valley Forge. *This page:* The National Park Service has carefully reconstructed the huts of George Washington's troops to interpret life during the winter of 1777–78. *Below:* Artillery Park, the area where cannon were originally massed, is one of two skillfully re-created aspects of the Revolutionary War scene at Valley Forge National Historical Park.

Washington Crossing State Park, north of Philadelphia along the Delaware River, is the site from which General Washington launched his famous crossing of the Delaware on Christmas Eve, 1776; one of the most important buildings is the Inn at McConkey's Ferry, believed to be where Washington and his aides dined before setting out for the Jersey shore. *Below:* A plaque commemorates all those who died from sickness and exposure before the Colonial troops crossed the Delaware River to fight the Battle of Trenton on Christmas Day, 1776. *Opposite:* A heroic statue of Washington standing in one of the Durham boats as it crossed the Delaware, marks the site of departure in Washington Crossing State Park.

The newly restored train station of the New Hope Railroad is the departure point for excursions on this old-time steam train. *Below:* The New Hope Barge Company transports passengers along a quiet and pastoral stretch of the Pennsylvania Canal in New Hope. *Opposite:* This house on Main Street in New Hope is one of a number of restored Victorian mansions in the town; many are now popular bed-and-breakfast establishments.

This bronze statue depicting Pickett's Charge is one of many on Gettysburg Battlefield that have been fully restored to their nineteenth-century brilliance. *Below:* General Robert E. Lee's headquarters at Gettysburg is just one stop on the many historical trails marked by the National Park Service at Gettysburg National Military Park. *Opposite:* The remains of 3,700 Union soldiers were reinterred in the Gettysburg National Cemetery a few years after the battle, and since that time as many veterans of more recent American conflicts have been laid to rest there.

The Battle of Gettysburg was the bloodiest engagement ever to be fought on American soil; this monument and hundreds of others commemorate the more than 50,000 men who were killed, wounded, or listed as missing in the battle. *Right:* The heroic statue of General Meade overlooks Gettysburg Battlefield; the domed Pennsylvania Memorial, honoring the nearly 35,000 commonwealth troops who fought here, is in the background.

Despite the coal and oil production in western Pennsylvania's hills, they retain their natural beauty. The Allegheny National Forest, one-half million acres of woodland with 200 miles of trails, is set right in the middle of the region. Hundreds of miles of winding roads penetrate the forest, connecting small towns and recreation sites.

East of the forest, the Laurel Highlands serve western Pennsylvanians as the Poconos serve those in the east. Canoers, kayakers, white-water rafters, and fishermen share crisp, cold mountain streams with brook, brown, and rainbow trout.

Up in Pennsylvania's sawed-off northwestern panhandle is the Lake Erie plain, with 32,000 acres of inland lakes and the 3,200-acre Presque Isle Peninsula wildlife refuge, which is home to more than 500 species of birds. The city of Erie prospers from the traffic into and out of its ports. A busy shipping and industrial town, Erie still manages to maintain the serene look of a resort center. This is a low-rise city planned along the lines of the nation's capital.

As Pennsylvanians stand on the brink of the twenty-first century, they are preparing to lead the nation in innovation. The first computer was invented at the University of Pennsylvania, the first electron microscope was invented in Allegheny County, and the first robotics institute was founded at Carnegie Mellon University. The history of the Keystone State runs from Ben Franklin's first bifocals to the super computer, from the country's first cookbook to the Constitution. Who knows what its future will bring?

Top: Once the mighty roar of steel furnaces echoed across the confluence of the Allegheny, Ohio, and Monongahela rivers in Pittsburgh; now silent—and much less polluted—the city has turned to more high-tech forms of industry. *Left:* At one time, just about every Pittsburgh family had someone who worked in the steel mills; today the fires have been put out due to competition from foreign steel sources. *Opposite:* The Heinz Memorial Chapel, known for its magnificent stained glass windows, is just one of a number of notable buildings on the University of Pittsburgh campus.

Pittsburgh sparkles on Light Up Night, the only night of the year when every light in the city is turned on; Point State Park, at the confluence of the Allegheny, Monongahela, and Ohio rivers is decorated with a giant Christmas tree. *Opposite:* The Pittsburgh Plate Glass Building, an all-glass-and-steel Gothic structure, has become a hallmark of the city's new skyline. *Overleaf:* The sun dips below the horizon behind the magnificent Pittsburgh skyline. Pittsburgh has enjoyed a recent renaissance of urban living that is the envy of many American cities.

Index of Photography

All photographs courtesy of The Image Bank, except where indicated *.